Color Heaven's Angels

Artwork by Donna Moses

HARVEST HOUSE PUBLISHERS
EUGENE, OREGON

Cover by Katie Brady Design, Eugene, Oregon

Scripture paraphrases are by the artist.

COLOR THE BIBLE is a registered trademark of The Hawkins Children's LLC. Harvest House Publishers, Inc., is the exclusive licensee of the federally registered trademark COLOR THE BIBLE.

COLOR HEAVEN'S ANGELS

Artwork copyright © Donna Moses
Published by Harvest House Publishers
Eugene, Oregon 97402
www.harvesthousepublishers.com

ISBN 978-0-7369-6873-7 (pbk.)

Printed in the United States of America

16 17 18 19 20 21 22 23 24 / VP-CD / 10 9 8 7 6 5 4 3 2 1

A Good Place to Begin

This coloring book is for artists of all ages and talents, and that means you! Let your creative spirit free, choose any color you like, and make each beautiful image your own. There are no rules except to have fun.

Enjoy the process. Feel free to use colored pencils, pens, watercolors, markers, and crayons—or any combination—to add color and texture to each design. Notice that all the pictures are printed on just one side of the paper. To keep colors from bleeding through to the next page, simply slip an extra piece of paper underneath the page you're working on. When finished, you might like to remove the page from the book, trim it to size, and frame your artwork for all to see.

Most importantly, have fun with the process. Enjoy experimenting with contrasting colors or different shades of the same color. Try lighter hues for a softer look, or layer and blend your colors for even more options. Allow some white space or saturate the entire piece with rich, vibrant color, depending on your mood. Let your worries go, relax in the moment, and allow your creative spirit to lead the way!

Rescue

The angels pulled Lot into the house, away from the wicked men who tried to break down his door, and urged him to run. "Take your wife and daughters and get out because judgment is coming on the city."

Genesis 19

Faith

Abraham's faith was stretched to the limit when God called him to sacrifice Isaac, his son of promise.
But suddenly an angel of the Lord shouted from heaven, "Do not hurt the boy!"
God had provided a substitute. GENESIS 22

The Blessing

The angel of the Lord spoke to Abraham a second time and said, "Since you did not withhold from Me your son, your only son, I will bless you and make your descendants as numerous as the stars in the sky and as the sand on the seashore. Your descendants will possess the cities of their enemies, and through your offspring all nations on the earth will be blessed because you obeyed Me."

GENESIS 22

Jacob

While Jacob was on his way to Haran, he came to a place where he stayed overnight because the sun had set. Using a stone to rest his head against, he dreamed that there was a ladder set up on earth that reached to heaven, and angels were ascending and descending on it.

GENESIS 28

God's Army

As Jacob went on his way with **people, flocks, herds, and camels,** God's angels met him. When Jacob saw them, he said, *"This is God's army!"* GENESIS 32

Moses

THE LORD WANTS TO USE YOU MOSES

An angel of the Lord appeared to Moses while he was shepherding a flock of sheep, and the Lord called to him out of a burning bush and said, "I am sending you to Pharaoh to bring the people of Israel out of Egypt." And Moses said, "Why me? What gives You the idea that I could ever do that?" And the Lord said, "I will be with you." EXODUS 3

Angels of Calamity

God's wrath against evil was displayed when He let loose the fierceness of His anger against Pharaoh. He sent angels of calamity on a mission, unleashing ten plagues that were to force Pharaoh to let His people go after 430 years of servitude. After the tenth plague, Moses was able to lead God's people forth like sheep and guide them to safety in confident trust.

EXODUS 7–12; PSALM 78:43-53

Go to a land flowing with
milk and *honey*

The Lord said to Moses, "Go, lead the people to the place of which I told you, the land
flowing with milk and honey, and I will send My angel to go before you."

EXODUS 33

Gideon

An angel of the Lord came and sat under the oak tree and spoke to Gideon while he was threshing wheat. "You are a mighty man of valor and a prospective savior of Israel," he said. Gideon protested about his utter weakness and inadequacy, not realizing that God turns man's weakness to strength when He commissions someone and says, "I will be with you." JUDGES 6

Elijah

The prophet Elijah was running for his life from Queen Jezebel when he came to a broom tree in the desert and lay down to rest. He prayed that he might die. Then he fell asleep, but an angel woke him up and gave him food and drink to restore his body before he continued to travel on. 1 Kings 19

Ezra

It was early morning when Ezra the priest stood before the people and prayed, "You are the Lord, You alone, and You made the heavens and all the angels, the earth and everything on it, the seas and everything in them. You preserve them all, and heaven's angels worship You." NEHEMIAH 9

King David

David celebrated God's favor that constantly surrounded him—just as it surrounds *all who reverence and worship* Him. Even in distress, there is always reason for praising and thanking God: *His angel encamps around* those who fear Him, and He delivers each of them. PSALM 34

donna moses

Angels

GLORY TO GOD

donna moses

The earth is crammed with *legions of God's holy angels,* tens of thousands and thousands of thousands...and the Lord is among them in the holy sanctuary in Jerusalem, just as He was at Sinai. PSALM 68

Praise Him

Let heaven's angels *praise Your wonders,* O Lord.
God's holy angels are in awe before You. Psalm 89:5

The Guardian

God has ordered His angels to
keep close watch and *guard*
His children, both young and old.

PSALM 91

God's Messengers

Bless the Lord,
you His angels, you mighty ones who do His
commandments, harkening to the voice of His word,
who do His pleasure in all places. Psalm 103

Comfort

The Lord is near to all who call upon Him sincerely and in truth. PSALM 145:18

The angel of the Lord found Hagar, the servant girl, near a spring in the desert and said, "I have heard and paid attention to your affliction, and I will multiply your descendants exceedingly so they will be too numerous to count." And Hagar said, "I have now seen the One who sees me." GENESIS 16; 21

PRAISE THE LORD, SUN, MOON, AND STARS OF LIGHT

Hallelujah

LET EVERYTHING THAT HAS THE BREATH OF LIFE, PRAISE THE NAME OF THE LORD! Psalm 148

PRAISE THE LORD FROM THE HEAVENS ~ PRAISE THE LORD, ALL HIS ANGELS

~ HALLELUJAH! PRAISE THE LORD FROM THE HEAVENS ~

Under Fire

Shadrach, Meshach, and Abednego, who served the Most High God, were thrown into the fiery furnace because they refused to serve King Nebuchadnezzar's gods or worship the golden image. But the fire had no power to harm their bodies because God sent an angel and delivered His servants who believed in Him, trusted in Him, and relied on Him. DANIEL 3

Daniel

Daniel said, "My God has sent His angel and has shut the lions' mouths so that they have not hurt me, because I was found innocent before Him and before King Darius."

DANIEL 6:22

Michael

NATIONAL GUARDIAN and PROTECTOR of ISRAEL

The archangel Michael is described as a *warrior angel* whom no hostile spirit force can overpower. He was the *national guardian angel* over Israel. DANIEL 10

Gabriel

MESSENGER AND INTERPRETER OF VISIONS

The archangel Gabriel appears in both the Old and New Testaments. He was the messenger angel who stood in the very presence of God. He delivered messages and interpreted visions and dreams of God's chosen people. LUKE 1

Zechariah

The archangel Gabriel appeared to Zechariah, a priest during the days when Herod was king of Judea, and said, "I have been sent to bring you good news. Your wife Elizabeth will give birth to a son, and you will call him John, and he will be great and distinguished in the sight of the Lord. He will be filled and controlled by the Spirit of God from his birth." The angel was referring to John the Baptist. LUKE 1

Mary

©donna moses

The archangel Gabriel said to Mary, "You have found grace with God. You shall become pregnant and give birth to a son, and you shall call His name Jesus. And of His reign there will be no end." When Mary questioned how this could happen since she was unmarried, Gabriel said, "No promise from God can fail to be fulfilled." LUKE 1

Shepherds

Suddenly an *angel of the Lord* appeared to the shepherds while they were watching their sheep by night. And the angel said, *"Do not be afraid."* LUKE 2:9-10

I BRING YOU GLAD TIDINGS OF GREAT JOY WHICH WILL COME TO ALL PEOPLE

Joy

Angels from the *realms of glory*,
Wing your flight o'er all the earth.
Ye who sang creation's story
Now proclaim *Messiah's birth.*

JOY TO THE WORLD

donna moses

The Promise

When God brought forth His firstborn Son into the world, He said,
"*Let all the angels worship Him.*" HEBREWS 1:6

When He Comes Again

The Son of Man is going to come with His **angels in the glory, majesty, and splendor** of His Father. And He will render account and reward everyone according to what they have done with their life.

MATTHEW 16:27

Keeping Watch

Jesus said, *"Be careful* that you don't treat one of these *little ones* in an unkind manner. Remember, angels who *keep watch over them* are constantly in touch with My *Father in heaven."* MATTHEW 18:10

Gethsemane

As Jesus went out of the city and up to the Mount of Olives, His disciples followed Him. When He reached His usual place, He fell on His knees and prayed these words: "Father, if You are willing, take this cup away from Me. But it is not My will, but Yours that must be done." Then an angel from heaven appeared to strengthen Him because He was in agony. Luke 22:39-43

He Is Not Here
He Has Risen

Near dawn on the first day of the week, Mary of Magdala and the other Mary went to the tomb.
There had been a great earthquake, for *an angel had rolled back the boulder* and sat upon it.
When the women arrived, he said to them, "He is not here; He has risen as He said He would do."

Matthew 28

GO INTO ALL THE WORLD AND TELL PEOPLE THE GOOD NEWS

GO INTO ALL THE WORLD AND TELL PEOPLE THE GOOD NEWS

Cornelius was a Roman centurion and the first Gentile convert to Christianity. In a vision, he clearly saw an angel of God, who said to him, "The Lord has heard your prayer and is about to help you. Send for Simon Peter to come to your house." When Peter arrived, he testified that everyone who believes in Jesus receives forgiveness of sins through His name. Cornelius and all his household believed and were baptized. Acts 10–11

Peter

Following the execution of the apostle James, Peter was arrested, imprisoned, and chained. He was awaiting execution himself, but prayer was made without ceasing by believers in Jerusalem. And while they were praying, God was working. Suddenly, an angel appeared, and a light shone in his cell. The angel woke Peter and said, "Get up quickly." Peter's chains fell off, and the angel led him out of the prison to freedom. ACTS 12

John

The apostle John had been exiled to the Isle of Patmos when an angel showed him what was to come in the near future. Overwhelmed by his words, John wanted to worship and pay divine honors to him, but the angel stopped him and said, "You must not do that. I am only a servant like you, John, who has accepted the testimony of Jesus. Worship God, for the essence of truth is the word of God." Revelation 19

Donna Moses has been painting her popular peasant folk art for more than four decades. She expresses traditional American values in charming collections illuminating faith, family, patriotism, and home that grace countless prints, calendars, stationery lines, and other licensed products. Mother of three and contemporary "Grandma Moses" to seven, Donna works out of her home studio in California.

We'd love to see your creations!
Share your finished projects on social media
with this hashtag:

#colorthebible

We'll be looking for your artwork!

For information on more
Harvest House coloring books for adults,
please visit our website:
www.harvesthousepublishers.com